SAUDI ARABIA 2013 HUMAN RIGHTS REPORT

EXECUTIVE SUMMARY

The Kingdom of Saudi Arabia is a monarchy ruled by King Abdullah bin Abdulaziz al-Saud, who is both head of state and head of government. The government bases its legitimacy on its interpretation of sharia (Islamic law) and the 1992 Basic Law, which specifies that the rulers of the country shall be male descendants of the founder King Abdulaziz bin Abdulrahman al-Saud. The Basic Law sets out the system of governance, rights of citizens, and powers and duties of the government, and it provides that the Koran and Sunna (the traditions of the Prophet Muhammad) serve as the country's constitution. In 2011 the country held elections on a nonparty basis for half of the 1,632 seats on the 285 municipal councils around the country. Independent polling station observers identified no irregularities with the election; however, women were not candidates and did not vote. While authorities generally maintained effective control over the security forces, there were some reports of human rights abuses by security forces.

The most important human rights problems reported included citizens' lack of the right and legal means to change their government; pervasive restrictions on universal rights such as freedom of expression, including on the internet, and freedom of assembly, association, movement, and religion; and a lack of equal rights for women, children, and noncitizen workers.

Other human rights problems reported included torture and other abuses; overcrowding in prisons and detention centers; holding political prisoners and detainees; denial of due process; arbitrary arrest and detention; and arbitrary interference with privacy, home, and correspondence. Violence against women, trafficking in persons, and discrimination based on gender, religion, sect, race, and ethnicity were common, although the government made efforts to counter discrimination in some areas and increasingly prosecuted individuals for trafficking and domestic violence. Lack of governmental transparency and access made it difficult to assess the magnitude of many reported human rights problems.

The government identified, prosecuted, and punished a limited number of officials who committed abuses, particularly those engaged in or complicit with corruption. Some members of the security forces and other senior officials reportedly committed abuses with relative impunity.

Section 1. Respect for the Integrity of the Person, Including Freedom from:

a. Arbitrary or Unlawful Deprivation of Life

The government or its agents were not known to have committed politically motivated killings during the year. Closed court proceedings in capital cases made it impossible to determine positively whether the accused were allowed to present a defense or were granted basic due process; however, in November 2012 the government amended the Law on Criminal Procedure to require a unanimous endorsement by the Supreme Judicial Council for all death sentences. Military and security courts investigated abuses of authority and security force killings.

In contrast with previous years, there were no reports that security forces killed persons during public demonstrations, although violence sometimes occurred.

On June 21, security forces killed Ali Hassan al-Mahrous, 19, a native of al-Khowayledeyah village near the city of Qatif in the Eastern Province. Al-Mahrous was waiting in a parked car on the side of the road at the time of his death when security forces, attempting to arrest another resident of Qatif, killed him in an exchange of gunfire with the other resident. Authorities closed the investigation regarding responsibility for the death after Mabahith (internal security forces) in Eastern Province threatened to bury his body in an unknown location rather than return it to his family if al-Mahrous' father continued to push for charges against the police.

According to the country's practice of sharia, capital punishment is the prescribed penalty for sorcery. Sorcery is distinguished from the practice of magic or witchcraft in that it necessarily involves an act or intent to inflict physical or psychological harm on another person. The country lacks a written penal code listing criminal offenses and the associated penalties for them (see section 1. e.); absent such a code, the punishments for the practice of magic or sorcery are subject to considerable judicial discretion in the courts. In contrast with 2012, there were no executions for sorcery during the year.

b. Disappearance

The government reportedly arrested and detained multiple persons during the year, refusing for extended periods in some cases to acknowledge the detention or to provide information about an individual's whereabouts. There were no reports, however, of politically motivated disappearances during the year.

c. Torture and Other Cruel, Inhuman, or Degrading Treatment or Punishment

The law prohibits torture and holds criminal investigation officers accountable for any abuse of authority. Sharia, as interpreted in the country, prohibits judges from accepting confessions obtained under duress; statutory law provides that public investigators shall not subject accused persons to coercive measures to influence their testimony.

Government officials claimed that Ministry of Interior rules prohibiting torture prevented such practices from occurring in the penal system. They also claimed representatives from the governmental Human Rights Commission (HRC) and the quasi-nongovernmental National Society for Human Rights (NSHR), supported by a trust funded by the estate of the late King Fahd, conducted prison visits to ascertain that torture did not occur in prisons or detention centers. Nevertheless, there continued to be reports that Ministry of Interior officials sometimes subjected prisoners and detainees to torture and other physical abuse, particularly during the investigation phase when interrogating suspects; however, due to lack of government transparency, it was not possible to ascertain the accuracy of these reports. There was no available information on the number of cases of abuse and corporal punishment.

In October the son of Khalid al-Rashid, detained by the government in a Ministry of Interior prison since 2007, reported his father's health was worsening as a result of a hunger strike and reports of torture in prison. Authorities arrested al-Rashid, the imam of a mosque in al-Khobar in the Eastern Province, for calling for protests in front of the headquarters of the Riyadh governorate over the lack of government response to the 2005 controversy over the Danish newspaper *Jyllands-Posten* cartoons of the Prophet Mohammed. Authorities charged al-Rashid with inciting the public against the government and imposed a five-year prison sentence that authorities later increased to 15 years.

In March authorities executed seven men for armed robbery and other crimes, despite claims by UN officials and Amnesty International that the men had possibly been tortured and their confessions coerced.

In 2011 security officials reportedly took human rights activist Mekhlef bin Daham al-Shammary from his prison cell at the Damman General Prison and allegedly poured an antiseptic cleaning liquid down his throat, resulting in his hospitalization. Officials released al-Shammary from prison in March 2012. On

February 17, al-Shammary asked the Specialized Criminal Court in Riyadh to complete proceedings against him after judicial authorities failed to issue a sentence by the February 10 deadline. Officials at the court reportedly told al-Shammary that it had postponed indefinitely issuing his sentence. In 2012 the Board of Grievances reportedly awarded al-Shammary compensation for wrongful detention. In November, however, an appeals court in Riyadh ruled that his case was not in the jurisdiction of the Board of Grievances.

In an unrelated case, the father of Khalid bin Fahad al-Shammary submitted a complaint in October 2012 to the Riyadh administrative court claiming his son died from torture and mistreatment following his arrest in Hail Province in 2006. The complaint named Mabahith officer Abdul Aziz al-Ahmadi as one of the perpetrators of the abuse and claimed al-Shammary died in the Security Forces Hospital in Riyadh, after deterioration of his medical condition resulting from abuse and denial of medical care. At year's end there was no action on the complaint.

The Commission for the Promotion of Virtue and Prevention of Vice (CPVPV), a semi-autonomous agency – referred to by some as the "religious police" – has the authority to monitor social behavior and enforce morality subject to the law and in coordination with law enforcement authorities.

The courts continued to use corporal punishment as a judicial penalty, almost always in the form of floggings. According to local human rights activists, police officials conduct the floggings according to a set of guidelines determined by local interpretation of sharia. The police official administering the punishment must place a book under his arm that prevents raising the hand above the head, limiting the ability to inflict pain on the person subjected to the punishment, and instructions forbid police from breaking the skin or causing scarring when administering the lashes. In contrast with 2012, there were no judicially administered amputations during the year. There was one execution by beheading.

Prison and Detention Center Conditions

Prison and detention center conditions varied, and some did not meet international standards.

Physical Conditions: The director general of prisons announced in February that there were 47,000 male and female prisoners and detainees in the kingdom, of whom noncitizens constituted approximately 72 percent. Authorities housed men and women in separate facilities and staffed women's prisons by female guards. Juveniles constituted less than 1 percent of detainees, according to a 2009 estimate. Although information on the maximum capacity of the facilities was not available, overcrowding in some detention centers was a problem. In a 2012 report published after visiting detention centers across the kingdom, the NSHR noted improvements in conditions at women's jails and detention centers, specifically women's detention centers in Mecca, following a visit to the facility in February 2012. Independent human rights activists, however, reported that foreign-national female guards at detention centers, in particular in al-Qassim Province, physically mistreated female detainees in a number of instances. Violations listed in the report included a shortage of, and improperly trained, wardens; lack of access to prompt medical treatment when requested; holding prisoners beyond the end of their sentences; and failure to inform prisoners of their legal rights. Some detained individuals complained about lack of access to adequate healthcare services.

On November 2, there was a fire at the Buraidah prison in al-Qassim Province; prisoners subsequently rioted, and at least four persons sustained injuries from gunshot wounds, bruises, and smoke inhalation.

Authorities held pretrial detainees together with convicted prisoners. They separated persons suspected or convicted of terrorism offenses from the general population but held them in similar facilities. There were no reports of prisoners denied access to potable water.

Activists alleged that authorities sometimes detained individuals in the same cells as individuals with mental disabilities as a form of punishment and indicated that authorities equally mistreated these persons with disabilities. On October 10, Abdulaziz al-Hussan, lawyer of detained activist Suliman al-Rashoodi, stated that al-Rashoodi planned to go on a hunger strike if authorities did not remove two mentally ill persons from his cell.

Administration: There were multiple legal authorities for prisons and detention centers. Local provincial authorities ran some prisons while the Ministry of Interior ran the others. Pretrial detainees sometimes were held in the same facilities as those detained postconviction, as there was no enforced policy in place to detain these two groups separately. Recordkeeping on prisoners was inadequate. There were reports that authorities held prisoners after they had completed their sentences. Penal and judicial authorities used alternatives to incarceration for nonviolent offenders, including probation, house arrest, travel bans, and religious counseling. In February, however, the Ministry of Interior launched an "electronic portal" that reportedly provided detainees and their relatives access to a database containing information about the legal status of the detainee, including any scheduled trial dates. No ombudsmen were available to register or investigate complaints made by prisoners, although prisoners could and did submit complaints to the HRC and the NSHR for investigation. Authorities differentiated between violent and nonviolent prisoners, pardoning nonviolent prisoners to reduce the prison population.

Authorities permitted relatives and friends to visit prisoners twice per week; however, there were reports that prison officials denied this privilege in some instances. Authorities permitted Muslim detainees and prisoners to perform religious observances. There was no information available whether prisoners were able to submit complaints to judicial authorities without censorship or whether authorities investigated credible allegations of inhuman conditions and treatment and made them public. The families of detainees could access a website for the Ministry of Interior General Directorate of Prisons that contained forms to apply for prison visits, temporary leave from prison (generally approved approximately during the post-Ramadan Eid holidays), and release on bail (for pretrial detainees). In October after the Eid al-Adha holiday, however, many family members of detained persons complained that authorities canceled scheduled visits with their relatives without reason.

Independent Monitoring: No independent human rights observers visited prisons or detention centers during the year. The government permitted foreign diplomats to visit prison facilities to view general conditions in a limited number of nonconsular cases; however, these visits were to view facilities rather than to meet with detainees. The most recent prison visit conducted by an independent human rights organization was a 2006 visit by Human Rights Watch; however, the government permitted the governmental HRC and domestic organizations such as the NSHR to monitor prison conditions. The organizations stated that they visited prisons throughout the country and reported on prison conditions. The NSHR monitored health care in prisons and brought deficiencies to the attention of the Ministry of Interior, which administers prisons and detention centers. In its 2012 annual report, the NSHR registered 861 cases involving prisoners and detainees who complained about conditions, compared with 759 cases in 2011.

Improvements: The most recently available statistics indicated there are 116 prison facilities run by the General Directorate of Prisons, including 12 reformatories; however, authorities expanded the prison system through the construction of new facilities during the year. In a 2012 report published after visiting eight detention centers across the kingdom, the NSHR reported some improvements in provision of medical services, education, and overall cleanliness. The report also noted increased complaints from detainees about visitation rights and observed that the government rented some prison buildings rather than owning them. This circumstance limited government efforts to improve prison infrastructure in some cases.

d. Arbitrary Arrest or Detention

The law provides that no entity may restrict a person's actions or imprison him, except under provisions of the law. A person under arrest legally may not be detained for more than 24 hours, except pursuant to a written order from a public investigator. Authorities must inform the detained person of the reasons for detention. Nonetheless, because of the government's ambiguous implementation of the law and a lack of due process, the Ministry of Interior, to which the majority of forces with arrest power report, maintained broad powers to arrest and detain persons indefinitely without judicial oversight or effective access to legal counsel or family. Authorities held persons for weeks, months, and sometimes years and reportedly failed to advise them promptly of their rights, including their legal right to be represented by an attorney.

Role of the Police and Security Apparatus

The king and the Ministries of Defense and Interior, in addition to the National Guard, are all responsible for law enforcement and maintenance of order. The Ministry of Interior exercises primary control over internal security and police forces. The civil police and the internal security police have authority to arrest and detain individuals.

The semiautonomous CPVPV, which monitors public behavior to enforce strict adherence to the official interpretation of Islamic norms, reports to the king via the Royal Diwan (royal court) and to the Ministry of Interior. The members of the CPVPV are required to carry official identification and have a police officer accompany them at the time of an arrest. On January 28, the king issued a royal decree curtailing some CPVPV powers, transferring responsibilities to other competent authorities. While the CPVPV may detain suspects for brief periods, it must transfer suspects directly to police authorities to complete legal proceedings against them. The head of the CPVPV, Sheikh Abdullatif Al al-Sheikh, stated in January that CPVPV agents have authority to investigate only certain categories of offenses, including harassment of women, alcohol and drug-related offenses, witchcraft, and sorcery. Al al-Sheikh said the new reforms, designed to harmonize the CPVPV's operations with the Law of Criminal Procedure, would be implemented fully and that CPVPV agents acting illegally would be punished. On November 13, the president of the CPVPV issued an executive bylaw prohibiting CPVPV employees from pursuing the vehicles of individuals suspected of engaging in activities in contravention of the country's interpretation of sharia. The circular directed the employees to note the license plate numbers of the vehicles and pass them to police patrols for further action. Authorities designed the bylaw to prevent road accidents as a result of such pursuits; it followed a highly publicized case in September when two men died in a car accident after being pursued by the CPVPV in Riyadh. At year's end CPVPV pursuits reportedly had decreased, but the CPVPV was not universally adhering to the regulations.

Ministry of Interior police and security forces were generally effective at maintaining law and order. The Board of Grievances (Diwan al-Mazalim), a high-level administrative judicial body that specializes in cases against government entities and reports directly to the king, is the only formal mechanism available to seek redress for claims of abuse. Citizens may report abuses by security forces at any police station, to the HRC, or to the NSHR. The HRC and the NSHR maintained records of complaints and outcomes, but privacy laws protected information about individual cases and information was not publicly available. During the year there were no reported prosecutions of security forces for human rights violations, but the Board of Grievances held hearings and adjudicated claims of wrongdoing. The HRC, in cooperation with the Ministry of Education, provided materials and training to police, security forces, and the CPVPV on protecting human rights.

The Bureau of Investigation and Prosecution (BIP) and the Control and Investigation Board (CIB) are the two units of the government with authority to investigate reports of criminal activity, corruption, and "disciplinary cases" involving government employees. These bodies are responsible for investigating potential cases and referring them to the administrative courts.

In 2011 the Council of Ministers consolidated legal authorities for investigation and public prosecution of criminal offences within the BIP; however, the CIB continued to be responsible for investigation and prosecution of noncriminal cases. All financial audit and control functions were limited to the General Auditing Board.

Arrest Procedures and Treatment While in Detention

According to the Law of Criminal Procedure, "no person shall be arrested, searched, detained, or imprisoned except in cases provided by law, and any accused person shall have the right to seek the assistance of a lawyer or a representative to defend him during the investigation and trial stages." Authorities may summon any person for investigation, and an arrest warrant may be issued based on evidence, but warrants frequently were not used, and they were not required in cases where probable cause existed.

The law requires that charges be filed within 72 hours of arrest and a trial within six months. Legally, authorities may not detain a person under arrest for more than 24 hours, except pursuant to a written order from a public investigator. Authorities reportedly often failed to observe these legal protections, and there was no requirement to advise suspects of their rights. Judicial proceedings began after authorities completed a full investigation, which in some cases took years.

There was a functioning bail system for less serious criminal charges. The law does not specify a timeframe for access to a lawyer. The state typically provided a lawyer for indigents.

Incommunicado detention was sometimes a problem. Authorities reportedly did not always respect detainees' right to contact family members following arrest. Security and some other types of prisoners sometimes remained in detention for long periods before family members or associates received information of their whereabouts. On January 6, authorities detained Khalid al-Natour, a Jordanian activist traveling through the Riyadh airport. Authorities did not charge al-Natour with a crime, nor did they inform him of the reasons for his detention. Nongovernmental organizations (NGOs) reported authorities did not allow al-Natour to contact his family or access a lawyer while detained. Authorities released him on April 7.

In response to protests by family members of long-term security detainees, many of whom were suspects held on terrorism or security grounds, in February the Ministry of Interior created a website designed to connect detainees with their families "for humanitarian reasons." According to the ministry, the government provides family members of detainees with usernames and passwords to access a website to send emails, make calls, and arrange direct video conferencing sessions with detainees. Detainees would also be able to use the new portal to apply for short periods of release to attend family weddings or funerals.

<u>Arbitrary Arrest</u>: There were reports of arbitrary arrest and detention. Although the law prohibits detention without charge for periods longer than six months, during the year authorities detained without charge security suspects, persons who publicly criticized the government, Shia religious leaders, and persons who violated religious standards.

<u>Pretrial Detention</u>: Lengthy pretrial detention was a problem. A local NGO, the Saudi Civil and Political Rights Association (ACPRA), challenged the Ministry of Interior publicly and in court on cases considered to involve arbitrary arrest or detention; however, ACPRA claimed the ministry ignored judges' rulings and judges appeared powerless to take action against the ministry. There was no available information on the percentage of the prison detainee population in pretrial detention or the average length of time held. Human rights activists reportedly received up to three calls per week from families claiming authorities held their relatives arbitrarily.

In March the Ministry of Interior's BIP released statistics accounting for those detained for suspicion of terrorism since 2001. The data indicated that of the 11,527 persons arrested on security grounds since 2001, authorities had released 8,755 (or approximately 75 percent). Of those released, according to the ministry, 551 were foreign nationals and 2,221 were Saudi citizens. Those not released had either been referred to "the competent criminal courts," or were still "being tried," according to previous announcements by the ministry. It was unclear what were the differences in these legal designations. In 2012 the ministry also reportedly paid compensation of 32 million riyals ($8.5 million) to 486 detainees for being held longer in detention than their jail sentences and provided 529 million riyals ($141 million) in monthly assistance to the families of suspects.

<u>Amnesty</u>: The king continued the tradition of commuting some judicial punishments. The details of the cases varied, but the demonstration of royal pardons sometimes included reducing or eliminating corporal punishment, for example, rather than setting aside the conviction. The remaining sentence could be added to a new sentence if the pardoned prisoner committed a crime subsequent to his release. This circumstance applied to ACPRA member Abdullah al-Hamid. In March authorities sentenced him to five years in prison and added six years from a previously suspended sentence, despite the fact that the amnesty from the king was final. There were general pardons or grants of amnesty on special occasions throughout the year. The Saudi Press Agency reported that authorities pardoned and released at least 1,543 prisoners during 2012. Additionally, the agency

reported pardons for 325 of 1,719 Indonesian prisoners during 2012. In August the king pardoned 57 prisoners in al-Qassim Province.

e. Denial of Fair Public Trial

The law provides that judges are independent and are subject to no authority other than the provisions of sharia and laws in force. Nevertheless, the judiciary was not independent, as it was required to coordinate its decisions with executive authorities, with the king as final arbiter. Although allegations of interference with judicial independence were rare, the judiciary reportedly was subject to influence. There were no reports during the year of courts exercising jurisdiction over senior members of the royal family, and it was not clear whether the judiciary would have jurisdiction in such instances. Allegedly, there were problems enforcing court orders, particularly against the Ministry of Interior.

Trial Procedures

The law states that defendants should be treated equally in accordance with sharia. In the absence of a written penal code listing criminal offenses and punishments, judges in the courts determine these penalties by legal interpretations of sharia. The Council of Senior Religious Scholars, an autonomous advisory body, issues religious opinions (fatwas) that guide how judges interpret sharia.

Additionally, sharia is not solely based on precedent. As a result, rulings and sentences can diverge widely from case to case. According to judicial procedures, appeals courts cannot independently reverse lower court judgments; they are limited to affirming judgments or returning them to a lower court for modification. Even when judges do not affirm judgments, appeals judges, in some cases, return the judgment to the judge who originally authored the opinion. This procedure sometimes makes it difficult for parties to receive a ruling that differs from the original judgment in cases where judges hesitate to admit error. Judges may base their decisions on any of the four Sunni schools of jurisprudence; however, the Hanbali School is predominant and forms the basis for the country's law and legal interpretations of sharia. Shia citizens use their legal traditions to adjudicate family law cases between Shia parties; however, either party can decide to adjudicate a case in state courts, which use Sunni legal tradition.

According to the law, there is neither presumption of innocence nor trial by jury. The law states that court hearings shall be public; however, courts may be closed at the judge's discretion, and as a result many trials during the year were closed.

According to the Ministry of Justice, authorities may close a trial depending on the sensitivity of the case to national security, the reputation of the defendant, or the safety of witnesses. Trials of suspected terrorist were nominally open to observers from the HRC, the media, and the public; however, observers required advance approval from the Ministry of Interior.

According to the HRC, the government may, at its discretion, provide an attorney to indigents at public expense. The law provides defendants the right to be present at trial and to consult with an attorney during the investigation and trial. There is no right to access government-held evidence. Defendants may request to review evidence and the court decides whether to grant the request. Defendants also have the right to confront or question witnesses against them and call witnesses on their behalf, but the court presents the witnesses. The law provides that an investigator appointed by the BIP questions the witnesses called by the litigants before the initiation of a trial and may hear testimony of additional witnesses he deems necessary to determine the facts. A defendant may not be compelled to take an oath or subjected to any coercive measures. The court must inform convicted persons of their right to appeal rulings.

Sharia as interpreted by the government extends these provisions to all citizens and noncitizens; however, the law and practice discriminate against women, nonpracticing Sunni, Shia, foreigners, and persons of other religions. For example, judges may discount the testimony of nonpracticing Sunni Muslims, Shia Muslims, or persons of other religions; sources reported that judges sometimes completely ignored testimony by Shia.

Among many reports of irregularities in trial procedures was the case of Mohammed Saleh al-Bajady, a political dissident and founding member of ACPRA. On August 14, a week after his release following more than two years in detention, authorities re-incarcerated him. Originally, authorities arrested al-Bajady in 2011 for his leadership role in ACPRA and for publicly demanding political and legal reforms, including calling for a constitutional monarchy in the kingdom and protection for freedom of expression and association. In April 2012 authorities sentenced him to four years' imprisonment and a subsequent five-year travel ban. During al-Bajady's trial, the court denied observers access to hearings and refused to allow his lawyer access to the courtroom. It was unclear whether al-Bajady would be required to serve the remainder of his four-year sentence.

In contrast with past practice, judicial authorities permitted local human rights activists to attend the trial of Eissa al-Nekhaify, whom authorities sentenced on

April 29 to three years in prison and a four-year travel ban for criticizing government authorities.

On January 9, authorities beheaded Rizana Nafeek, a Sri Lankan domestic worker convicted of having killed a four-month-old infant, Naif al-Quthaibi, in 2005. The execution followed the refusal by the infant's parents to agree to a pardon or to accept blood money in compensation for the death despite the intervention of high-ranking officials, including Crown Prince Salman. Local human rights activists claimed Nafeek was a minor at the time of the crime and denied due process by not having an interpreter during her interrogation and trial. In a circular issued to diplomatic missions, the government refuted allegations that Nafeek was a legal minor, citing that her official passport stated that she was 21 years old at the time she committed the crime and that her passport was an official document issued by her government. The government further stated that the law does not allow recruitment of minors for domestic labor. The circular asserted that Nafeek received all rights for a legal defense under the supervision of the Sri Lankan embassy in Riyadh and that the government cooperated with all requests by the Sri Lankan government, including facilitating the visit to Riyadh of high-ranking Sri Lankan delegations to discuss the case, among them the Sri Lankan attorney general.

Political Prisoners and Detainees

The number of political prisoners or detainees who reportedly remained in prolonged detention without charge could not be reliably ascertained.

In many cases it was impossible to determine the legal basis for incarceration and whether the detention complied with international norms and standards. Those who remained imprisoned after trial were often convicted of terrorism-related crimes, and there was not sufficient public information about such alleged crimes to judge whether they had a credible claim to be political prisoners. The Specialized Criminal Court tried a small number of political prisoners each year for actions unrelated to terrorism or violence against the state.

International NGOs, in particular Amnesty International, criticized the government for abusing its antiterrorism prerogatives to arrest some members of the political opposition. Authorities generally gave security detainees the same protections as other prisoners or detainees. High-profile prisoners generally were well treated. Certain prisoners, held on terrorism-related charges, had the option of participating in government-sponsored rehabilitation programs. Authorities sometimes restricted legal access to detainees; no international humanitarian organizations had access to them.

In July an appeals court increased the prison sentence of Shia cleric Tawfiq al-Aamer from three years in prison to four years and upheld al-Aamer's five-year travel ban. Detained in 2011 for comments critical of the government, authorities charged al-Aamer in November 2012 with calling for political change, libeling the country's religious scholars, and collecting illegal religious donations, among other offenses.

In July 2012 security forces arrested Shia cleric Nimr al-Nimr, who sustained a gunshot wound to his left leg in the process; no charges were known to have been filed against him. Following his arrest al-Nimr went on a 45-day hunger strike; after medical treatment and a hospital stay, authorities transferred him to Ha'ir prison outside Riyadh. In March the public prosecutor in the BIP asked for al-Nimr to be sentenced, executed, and his body publicly crucified for spreading heresy, inciting sectarian dissent, interfering in the affairs of other countries, and meeting with wanted criminals. Authorities allowed family members to visit al-Nimr at Ha'ir prison, where he remained at year's end.

Civil Judicial Procedures and Remedies

Complainants claiming human rights violations generally sought assistance from the HRC or NSHR, which either advocated on their behalf or provided courts with opinions on their cases. The HRC was generally responsive to complaints; domestic violence cases were the most common. Individuals or organizations also may petition directly for damages or government action to end human rights violations before the Board of Grievances except in compensation cases related to state security where the Specialized Criminal Court handles remediation.

In some cases the government did not carry out in a timely manner judicially ordered compensation for unlawful detentions. On February 27, the Specialized Criminal Court awarded Abdulrahman al-Dosary compensation of 350,000 riyals ($93,330) for detention for 102 days in excess of his sentences; however, as of year's end, the award had not been paid.

f. Arbitrary Interference with Privacy, Family, Home, or Correspondence

The law prohibits unlawful intrusions into the privacy of persons, their homes, places of work, and vehicles. Criminal investigation officers are required to maintain records of all searches conducted; these records should contain the name of the officer conducting the search, the text of the search warrant (or an explanation of the urgency that necessitated the search without a warrant), and the names and signatures of the persons who were present at the time of search. While the law also provides for the privacy of all mail, telegrams, telephone conversations, and other means of communication, the government did not respect the privacy of correspondence or communications, and the government used the considerable latitude provided by the law to monitor activities legally and intervene where it deemed necessary.

There were reports from human rights activists of governmental monitoring or blocking mobile telephone or internet usage before planned demonstrations. The government strictly monitored politically related activities and took punitive actions, including arrest and detention, against persons who engaged in certain political activities, such as direct public criticism of some senior royals by name, forming a political party, or organizing a demonstration. Customs officials reportedly routinely opened mail and shipments to search for contraband. In some areas Ministry of Interior informants allegedly reported "seditious ideas," "antigovernment activity," or "behavior contrary to Islam" in their neighborhoods.

The CPVPV monitored and regulated public interaction between members of the opposite sex.

Section 2. Respect for Civil Liberties, Including:

a. Freedom of Speech and Press

Civil law does not protect human rights, including freedom of the speech and of the press; only local interpretation and the practice of sharia law protect these rights, and there were frequent reports of restrictions of free speech. The Basic Law specifies that "mass media and all other vehicles of expression shall employ civil and polite language, contribute towards the education of the nation, and strengthen unity. The media is prohibited from committing acts that lead to disorder and division, affect the security of the state or its public relations, or undermine human dignity and rights." Authorities are responsible for regulating and determining which speech or expression undermines internal security.

The Press and Publications Law states that violators can be fined up to 500,000 riyals ($133,300) for each violation of the law, which is doubled if the violation is repeated. Other penalties include banning individuals from writing. Formally, the

Violations Considerations Committee in the Ministry of Culture and Information has responsibility for the law; however, sharia court judges, who consider these issues regularly, exercised wide discretion in interpreting the law, which made it unclear which expression accords with the law.

Government-friendly ownership of print or broadcast media led to self-censorship, and there was relatively little need for overt government action to restrict freedom of expression. The government, however, could not rely on self-censoring in social media and the internet. Accordingly, to control information, it monitored and blocked certain internet sites. On a number of occasions, government officials and senior clerics publicly warned against inaccurate reports on the internet and reminded the public that criticism of the government and its officials should be done through available private channels. The government charged those using the internet to express dissent with subversion, blasphemy, and apostasy.

Freedom of Speech: The government monitored public expressions of opinion and took advantage of legal controls to impede the free expression of opinion and restrict those verging on the political sphere. The government prohibits public employees from directly or indirectly engaging in dialogue with local or foreign media or participating in any meetings intended to oppose state policies. The law forbids apostasy and blasphemy, which legally can carry the death penalty, although there have not been any modern instances of death sentences for these crimes. Statements construed by authorities to constitute defamation of the king, monarchy, governing system, or the al-Saud family have resulted in criminal charges for several Saudis advocating government reform.

The government charged a number of individuals with crimes related to their exercise of free speech during the year. On October 2, human rights lawyer and activist Waleed Abu al-Khair was taken into custody in Jeddah after holding an "unauthorized gathering" to discuss political affairs. On December 14, a judge sentenced Umar al-Sa'id, a member of ACPRA, to 300 lashes and four years in prison for calling for a constitutional monarchy and criticizing the country's human rights record. Authorities released him on bail on October 3.

On October 6, court authorities charged Abu al-Khair with seeking to overthrow the head of state, tarnishing the reputation of the judiciary, inciting international organizations against the kingdom, forming an unlicensed human rights society, participating in the activities of an organization unlicensed in Saudi Arabia, and attempting to set public opinion against the king. According to Abu al-Khair's wife, authorities targeted him due to his relations with political reformists. The

BIP sought a sentence of five years imprisonment and the closing of his online social media accounts. In June 2012 a Jeddah court charged Abu al-Khair with "tarnishing" the image of the kingdom and contempt of the judiciary, and he was held in detention for three months. In September 2011 authorities charged Abu al-Khair, who also supervised the Facebook group Saudi Human Rights Monitor, with criticizing the government. He has been subjected to an indefinite travel ban since 2011.

On June 5, authorities released author and commentator Turki al-Hamad into the custody of his family after six months of detention without charge. Authorities detained al-Hamad in December 2012 after he published Twitter comments critical of Islamists and political Islam. The Riyadh-based NGO Global Commission for Introducing the Messenger claimed it originally requested that the interior minister detain al-Hamad for his controversial comments.

On July 29, a court sentenced Ra'if Badawi to seven years in prison and 600 lashes for violating Islamic values, breaking sharia law, blasphemy, and mocking religious symbols using a website. The presiding judge also ordered the internet forum closed, although it had been inactive since June 2012. A human rights activist and the founder of the online social forum Saudi Liberals Network, Badawi was detained in June 2012 after his father charged him with "disobedience" in connection with the online forum. At year's end Badawi remained in custody; an appeal of his sentence continued.

On October 29, authorities released blogger Hamza Kashgari to the custody of his family. In February 2012 authorities arrested him in Malaysia and returned him to the country on charges of blasphemy after he published a poem on Twitter deemed insulting to the Prophet Mohammed.

Press Freedoms: The Press and Publications Law, which extends explicitly to internet communications, governs printed materials; printing presses; bookstores; the import, rental, and sale of films; television and radio; and foreign media offices and their correspondents. In 2011 a royal decree amended the law to strengthen penalties and created a special commission to judge violations. The decree bans publishing anything "contradicting sharia; inciting disruption; serving foreign interests that contradict national interests; and damaging the reputation of the Grand Mufti, members of the Council of Senior Religious Scholars, or senior government officials." The Ministry of Culture and Information may permanently close "whenever necessary" any means of communication – defined as any means of expressing any viewpoint that is meant for circulation – that it deems is engaged in a prohibited activity as set forth in the 2011 royal decree. Print and broadcast media, already self-censored, did not appear demonstrably affected by these restrictions.

The government owned most print and broadcast media and book publication facilities in the country, and members of the royal family owned or influenced privately owned and nominally independent operations, including various media outlets and widely circulated pan-Arab newspapers such as *Ash-Sharq al-Awsat* and a*l-Hayat*. The government owned, operated, and censored most domestic television and radio outlets.

Satellite dish usage was widespread. Although satellite dishes are technically illegal, the government did not enforce restrictions on satellite dishes. Access to foreign sources of information, including the internet, was common. Privately owned satellite television networks headquartered outside the country maintained local offices and operated under a system of self-censorship. Many foreign satellite stations broadcast a wide range of programs into the country, in English and Arabic, including foreign news channels such as CNN, Fox, BBC, Sky, and al-Jazeera. Foreign media are subject to licensing requirements from the Ministry of Culture and Information and cannot operate freely.

The Ministry of Culture and Information must approve the appointment of all senior editors and has authority to remove them. The government provides guidelines to newspapers regarding controversial issues. A 1982 media policy statement urges journalists to uphold Islam, oppose atheism, promote Arab interests, and preserve cultural heritage. The Saudi Press Agency reports official government news.

All newspapers in the country must be government-licensed. Media outlets legally can be banned or have their publication temporarily halted if the government concludes they violated the Press and Publications Law.

Censorship or Content Restrictions: The government reportedly penalized those who published items counter to government guidelines and directly or indirectly censored the media by licensing domestic media and by controlling importation of foreign printed material. Authorities prevented or delayed the distribution of foreign print media, effectively censoring these publications. In some cases, however, individuals criticized specific government bodies or actions publicly without repercussions.

In September Prince al-Waleed bin Talal, as owner of the Rotana Group, a pan-Arab media conglomerate based in Riyadh, dismissed Kuwaiti national Tariq al-Suwaidan as director of the Islamic television channel *al-Risala* (The Message) because of the latter's public support for the Muslim Brotherhood and former Egyptian president Mohammed Morsi.

In 2011 authorities dismissed Fahad al-Aqran, the editor in chief of *al-Madina*, and Abdulaziz al-Sowaid, a columnist for *al-Madina*, and referred them to the Ministry of Culture and Information's review board after the columnist wrote an article with controversial interpretations of theological issues. They resumed their positions during the year.

The Consultative Council (Majlis as-Shura), an advisory body, frequently allowed print and broadcast media to observe its proceedings and meetings, but the council closed some high profile or controversial sessions to the media. For example, in May 2012 media reported that the council sat in closed session with the minister of labor to discuss introduction of a minimum wage and other labor issues.

Internet Freedom

There were government restrictions on access to the internet and credible reports the government monitored e-mails and internet chat rooms. Activists complained of monitoring or attempted monitoring of their communications on web-based communications applications. Internet access was widely available to and used by citizens of the country. The Press and Publications Law implicitly covers the electronic media, since it extends to any means of expression of a viewpoint meant for circulation, ranging from words to cartoons, photographs, and sounds. In 2011 the government issued "Implementing Regulations of Electronic Publishing," setting rules for internet-based and other electronic media, including chat rooms, personal blogs, and text messages. Security authorities actively monitored internet activity.

The Press and Publications Law criminalizes the publication or downloading of offensive sites. The governmental Communications and Information Technology Commission (CITC) filtered and blocked access to websites it deemed offensive, including pages calling for political, social, or economic reforms or human rights. In addition to blocking the websites of local and international human rights NGOs in the country, during the year authorities also blocked access to the websites of expatriate Saudi dissidents such as Ali al-Demainy and the website for the October

26 Women's Driving Campaign. Security regulations require internet cafe owners to install cameras and maintain records on their users.

On June 24, the Specialized Criminal Court found seven Shia men from al-Hasa in the Eastern Province guilty of charges that included "joining the so-called 'Movement of March 4th in al-Hasa' and the 'al-Hasa Freedom Movement,'" both of which maintained active Facebook pages. Authorities also charged two of the defendants with supporting and disseminating the views of London-based antiregime activist Sa'ad al-Faqih, a Saudi dissident who fled the kingdom in 1994. The court found the men guilty of violating the Anti-Cyber Crimes Law, which criminalizes the "production, preparation, transmission, or storage of material impinging on public order, religious values, public morals, and privacy." The men received prison sentences ranging from five to 10 years, as well as subsequent bans on their travel abroad.

The Ministry of Culture and Information or its agencies must authorize all websites registered and hosted in the country. The CITC dealt with requests to block adult content and coordinated decisions with the Saudi Arabian Monetary Agency on blocking phishing sites seeking to obtain confidential personal or financial information. Under the Telecommunication Act, failure by service providers to block banned sites can result in a fine of five million riyals ($1.33 million). All other requests to block sites were submitted to an interagency committee, chaired by the Ministry of Interior, for a decision to block a site or not. In addition to designating unacceptable sites, the CITC accepted requests from citizens to block or unblock sites. According to the CITC, authorities received an average of 200 requests daily to block and unblock sites. According to the NGO Reporters Without Borders, authorities claimed to have blocked cumulatively approximately 400,000 websites. CITC claimed Facebook removed materials the CITC deemed offensive, but Twitter ignored all CITC requests.

On June 5, the CITC announced its decision to block Viber, a proprietary cross-platform, voice-over-internet protocol application developed primarily for use on smart phones, for its failure to meet domestic "regulatory requirements." The announcement also warned that the CITC would "take appropriate action" against other applications or services, including Skype and WhatsApp, if the proprietary services did not allow the government "lawful access" for monitoring purposes. As of year's end, while the CITC refrained from action against Skype and WhatsApp, Viber remained inaccessible in the country without the use of a virtual private network.

Access to the internet was legally available only through government-authorized internet service providers. Although the authorities blocked websites offering proxies, persistent internet users could work around the blocked sites and continue to access the internet via other proxy servers.

Laws criminalize defamation on the internet, hacking, unauthorized access to government websites, and stealing information related to national security, as well as the creation or dissemination of a website for a terrorist organization. The government reportedly collected personally identifiable information concerning the identity of persons peacefully expressing political, religious, or ideological opinions or beliefs.

Academic Freedom and Cultural Events

The government censored public artistic expression, prohibited cinemas, and restricted public musical or theatrical performances apart from those considered folkloric and special events approved by the government. Academics reportedly practiced self-censorship, and authorities prohibited professors and administrators at public universities from hosting meetings at their universities with foreign academics or diplomats without prior government permission.

In August authorities in the Eastern Province canceled a dinner forum in Jubail hosted by local activists calling for the peaceful coexistence of the Sunni and Shia sects of Islam. Authorities gave no reason for the cancellation.

In some cases academics retained personal freedom of expression. During the year authorities did not terminate Mohammed al-Qahtani, a professor at the Ministry of Foreign Affairs Diplomatic Institute, despite his high-profile trial and subsequent conviction for founding an unlicensed organization. Al-Qahtani did not lose his pension despite the controversial nature of his case, and his official status at the institute did not change.

b. Freedom of Peaceful Assembly and Association

The law does not provide for freedom of assembly and association, which the government strictly limited.

Freedom of Assembly

The law requires a government permit for an organized public assembly of any type, and it forbids participation in political protests or unauthorized public assemblies. Security forces reportedly arrested demonstrators and detained them for brief periods.

As in 2012, however, security forces allowed more frequent small, unauthorized demonstrations throughout the country, despite a 2011 Ministry of Interior statement that demonstrations were banned and that it would take "all necessary measures" against those seeking to "disrupt order." In 2011 the Council of Senior Religious Scholars reinforced the government's stance, stating "demonstrations are prohibited in this country" and explaining that "the correct way in sharia of realizing common interests is by advising."

Throughout the year authorities continued to allow regular demonstrations in the Eastern Province city of Qatif. Activists reported that security forces used intimidation to discourage people from joining demonstrations as a general practice. There were also reports of security forces firing bullets in the air to disperse crowds. Videos posted on YouTube purported to portray residents, largely Shia, protesting alleged systematic discrimination and neglect in public investment while showing antiregime slogans written on walls.

On June 10, approximately 50 women in five cities conducted separate "freedom sit-ins" in Buraidah, Riyadh, Mecca, Hail, and al-Jowf. In the largest protest in Buraidah in al-Qassim Province, which involved 32 women, the protesters raised banners with the names and pictures of human rights defenders and male relatives detained on terrorism charges, shouted slogans criticizing the arrests, and called for their trial or release. In response to the protest, security forces arrested the demonstrators and 11 children who were present with them at the site; however, by year's end authorities had released nearly all from detention.

Freedom of Association

The law does not provide for freedom of association, and the government strictly limited this right. The government prohibited the establishment of political parties or any group it considered as opposing or challenging the regime. All associations must be licensed by the Ministry of Social Affairs and comply with its regulations. Some groups that advocated changing elements of the social or political order reported that their licensing requests went unanswered for years despite repeated inquiries. The ministry reportedly used arbitrary means, such as requiring unreasonable types and quantities of information, effectively denying licenses to associations. As of year's end, the Council of Ministers had not acted on a proposed law on NGOs, which the Consultative Council endorsed in 2008. The law only provides for the establishment of philanthropic and charitable societies. Organizations that have social or research mandates require royal backing to avoid government interference or prosecution.

On March 9, a Riyadh criminal court sentenced political activists Mohammed al-Qahtani and Abdullah al-Hamid, both members of ACPRA, with establishing and operating an unlicensed NGO. Activists established ACPRA in 2009 to call for increased political rights in the kingdom and to advocate and provide legal assistance for victims of human rights abuses, including those held in long-term detention on terrorism charges. The court sentenced al-Qahtani to 10 years in prison, to be followed by a 10-year travel ban. Abdullah al-Hamid received a five-year jail sentence in addition to six years from a previously suspended sentence. The court also sentenced him to a subsequent five-year travel ban. Authorities also charged them with publicly criticizing national leaders and accusing the government of human rights violations. The judge further ordered the immediate dissolution of ACPRA, confiscation of its assets, and closure of its website and social media accounts.

Government-chartered associations observed citizen-only limitations. For example, the Saudi Journalists Association, operating under a government charter, prohibited noncitizen members from voting and from attending the association's general assembly.

c. Freedom of Religion

See the Department of State's *International Religious Freedom Report* at www.state.gov/j/drl/irf/rpt.

d. Freedom of Movement, Internally Displaced Persons, Protection of Refugees, and Stateless Persons

The law does not contain provisions for freedom of internal movement, foreign travel, emigration, and repatriation. The government cooperated with the Office of the UN High Commissioner for Refugees (UNHCR) and other humanitarian organizations in providing protection and assistance to internally displaced persons, refugees, returning refugees, asylum seekers, stateless persons, and other persons of concern.

In-country Movement: The government generally did not restrict the free movement of male citizens within the country or the right of citizens to change residence or workplace, provided they held a national identification card (NIC). The law requires all male citizens 15 years old or older to hold a NIC. In November 2012 the Ministry of Interior announced it would start issuing NICs to all female citizens at 15 years of age, phasing in the requirement over a seven-year period. In September the ministry stated that it had issued only 1.5 million NICs since 2002 to women; the country's female population is approximately 9.8 million.

The guardianship system requires a woman to have the permission of her male guardian (normally a father, husband, son, brother, grandfather, uncle, or other male relative) to move freely in the country. The government limited driving licenses to men, which effectively prohibited women from driving motor vehicles. On October 26, between 41 and 80 women drove in a number of cities throughout the country in defiance of the prohibitions on women driving despite an October 24 Ministry of Interior statement that authorities would punish violators of the law. On October 26, police stopped between 15 and 20 women for driving; authorities fined each 300 riyal ($80). Police required each woman driver and her male guardian to pledge to "respect the kingdom's laws" before releasing them.

Foreign Travel: There are restrictions on foreign travel, including for women and members of minority groups. No one may leave the country without an exit visa and a passport. Women under the age of 45, minors (men younger than age 21), and other dependents or foreign citizen workers under sponsorship require a male guardian's consent to travel abroad. A noncitizen wife needs permission from her husband to travel unless both partners sign a prenuptial agreement permitting the noncitizen wife to travel without the husband's permission. Government entities and male family members can "blacklist" women and minor children, prohibiting their travel. The male guardian legally is able in custody disputes to prevent even adult children from leaving the country.

In April 2012 the Ministry of Interior began allowing male citizens to use the ministry's website to register electronic travel permits for their dependents and sponsored workers. Previously, applicants could request travel permits only from branches of the Passport Directorate, and dependents had to present the permits to passport officers upon exiting the country. As part of the new internet-based system, authorities notify all registrants by text message to their cell phone whenever a dependent or sponsored foreign citizen worker exits or enters the country. The notification service, an elective service when initiated in 2010, became automatic for all enrollees on the ministry's website in November 2012.

Employers or sponsors controlled the departure of foreign workers and residents from the country; employers/sponsors were responsible for processing residence permits and exit visas on their behalf. Sponsors frequently held their employees' passports against the desires of the employees, despite a law specifically prohibiting this practice. Typically, foreign workers provide sponsors with their residence permit (iqama) before traveling in exchange for their passport to ensure the worker's return to their employer after their travel. The government continued to impose travel bans as part of criminal sentences. The government on occasion reportedly confiscated passports and revoked the rights of some citizens to travel for political reasons but often did not provide them with notification or opportunity to contest the restriction.

During the year the government banned at least 20 individuals engaged in human rights activism or political activities from foreign travel. These included Shia cleric Tawfiq al-Aamer, human rights lawyer Waleed Abu al-Khair, activist Umar al-Sa'id, and journalist Iman al-Qahtani. The government banned at least 60 Shia leaders from traveling for more than two months between May and July after they signed a letter denouncing the government's arrest of Shia accused of spying for Iran.

Protection of Refugees

Access to Asylum: The law provides that the "state will grant political asylum if public interest so dictates." The country has no regulations implementing this provision, and the UNHCR managed refugee and asylum matters. The government permitted UNHCR-recognized refugees to stay in the country temporarily pending identification of a durable solution. The government generally did not grant asylum or accept refugees for settlement from third countries. Government policy is not to grant refugee status to persons in the country illegally, including those who have overstayed a pilgrimage visa. The government strongly encouraged persons without residency to leave, and it threatened or imposed deportation. Access to naturalization was difficult for refugees. In 2012 there were 588 refugees registered with the UNHCR. During 2012, 12 individuals applied for asylum. The majority of asylum seekers were Iraqi nationals, with smaller numbers of Syrians and Eritreans.

Employment: Refugees and asylum seekers are unable to work legally.

Access to Basic Services: The government reserves for citizens only the access to education, health care, public housing, courts and judicial procedures, legal services, and other social services. The UNHCR office in Riyadh provided a subsistence allowance covering basic services to a limited number of vulnerable families based on a needs assessment.

Stateless Persons

The country had a significant number of habitual residents who are legally stateless, but data on the stateless population were incomplete and scarce.

Under the Nationality Law, citizenship is derived from the father, but several scenarios lead to stateless children: (1) A child born to an unmarried mother is not affiliated with the father legally, even if the father has recognized the child, and therefore is stateless; (2) when identification documents are withdrawn from a parent, the child also loses his or her identification and accompanying rights (possible when a naturalized parent denaturalizes voluntarily or loses citizenship through other acts); (3) children of a citizen mother and a noncitizen father are without nationality, unless they acquire citizenship from the father; and (4) children of a citizen father and a noncitizen mother are noncitizens, unless the government has authorized the marriage of the parents prior to birth. Additionally, when government authorities withdraw a citizen's NIC, his or her children also lose their citizenship.

In September the government clarified regulations governing the status of non-Saudi men married to Saudi women. Male spouses of female citizens are entitled to permanent residency in the kingdom without needing a sponsor, and they receive free government education and medical benefits. These spouses also are entitled to count towards the "Nitaqaat" or Saudization percentage in the private sector, which improves their employment prospects. Non-Saudi wives of Saudi men in the kingdom receive more rights if they have children resulting from their marriage with a Saudi man than if they do not.

The UNHCR unofficially estimated there were approximately 70,000 stateless persons in the country, almost all of whom were native-born Arab residents known locally as Bidoon (an Arabic word that means "without" [citizenship]).

Bidoon are persons whose ancestors failed to obtain nationality, such as descendants of nomadic tribes not counted among the native tribes during the reign of the country's founder, King Abdulaziz; descendants of foreign-born fathers who arrived before there were laws regulating citizenship; and rural migrants whose parents failed to register their births. As noncitizens, Bidoon are unable to obtain passports or travel abroad. The government denied them employment and educational opportunities and their marginalized status made them among the poorest residents of the country. In recent years the Ministry of Education encouraged them to attend school. The government issues Bidoon five-year residency permits to facilitate their social integration in government-provided health care and other services, putting them on similar footing with sponsored foreign workers.

There were also some Baloch, West Africans, and several hundred thousand Rohingya Muslims from Burma; however, only a portion of these communities was stateless. For example, many Rohingya had expired passports that their home governments refused to renew. The UNHCR also estimated there were between 250,00 and 500,000 individuals of Burmese origin in the kingdom; some of these individuals are eligible to benefit from a program to correct their residency status; however, at year's end, it was unclear how many had received residency permits. Only an estimated 2,000 individuals of Rohingya origin had Saudi citizenship. There also were approximately 290,000 Palestinian residents not registered as refugees.

Section 3. Respect for Political Rights: The Right of Citizens to Change Their Government

The law does not provide citizens the right to change their government peacefully and establishes the al-Saud family monarchy as the political system. The law provides citizens the right to communicate with public authorities on any matter, and the government is established on the principle of consultation (shura). The king and senior officials, including ministers and regional governors, are required to make themselves available by holding meetings (majlis), open-door events where in theory any male citizen or noncitizen may express an opinion or a grievance without the need for an appointment. Most government ministries and agencies had women's sections to interact with female citizens and noncitizens, and at least two regional governorates hired female employees to receive women's petitions and arrange meetings for women with complaints for, or requests of, the governor. Only a few members of the ruling family have a voice in the choice of leaders, the composition of the government, or changes to the political system.

The Allegiance Commission, composed of up to 35 senior princes appointed by the king, is responsible for selecting a king and crown prince upon the death or incapacitation of either.

Elections and Political Participation

Recent Elections: In 2011 following a two-year postponement, the government held elections for the second time since 1963 for the country's 285 municipal councils. Elected candidates filled half of the 1,632 seats, while the king appointed the other half. As in the first elections in 2005, participation was limited to civilian male citizens at least 21 years old. Uniformed members of the security forces, including the military and police, were ineligible to vote. According to the Municipal Council Elections Committee, there was no legal prohibition against women voting; however, as in 2005, the committee cited logistical and other technical reasons to explain why women were not allowed to vote or run for office. More than 1,700 lawyers from the National Committee of Lawyers monitored the elections nationally, and the organization assessed that the elections were fair and transparent. The NSHR, however, refused to observe the elections, protesting women's ineligibility to vote or seek election. Election regulations prohibited candidates from contesting under party affiliation.

Political Parties: There were no political parties or similar associations. The law does not protect the right of individuals to organize politically.

In 2011 nine individuals requested recognition of the Islamic Nation Party (Hizb al-Umma al-Islami) as a political party. Authorities subsequently arrested seven of the party's nine founders and demanded that the founders sign a legally binding promise to withdraw their names from the party's founding document. All members of the group except Abdulaziz al-Wuhaibi signed the statement; authorities released them. The court sentenced al-Wuhaibi to seven years in prison. In November 2012 the appeals court for the Specialized Criminal Court overturned his sentence as too lenient and ordered a retrial. In December 2012 the authorities ordered al-Wuhaibi to undergo a psychological evaluation to determine whether he was responsible for the commission of any crime. In May authorities judged him innocent of any crime and transferred him to a psychological hospital. At year's end he remained in the hospital, where it was unclear whether he was detained in accordance with or against his will.

Participation of Women and Minorities: Discrimination based on widespread gender segregation excluded women from many aspects of public life, including from formal decision-making positions. Nevertheless, women increasingly participated in political life, albeit with significantly less status than men did. On January 11, the king issued a royal decree changing the governance of the Consultative Council, the 150-person royally appointed body, which advises the king and can propose laws. The changes mandate that women constitute no less than 20 percent of the membership of the Consultative Council. In accordance with the new law, the council inducted 30 women as full members on February 19.

In 2011 the king issued a royal decree granting women the right to vote and run as candidates in the next municipal council elections, scheduled for 2015.

There were no women on the High Court (women's ability to practice law is severely limited) or Supreme Judicial Council. There were no women judges or prosecutors. In contrast with previous years, on October 6, the Ministry of Justice granted four women a license to practice law in the kingdom. These licenses were the first to entitle women to argue cases before domestic courts.

There were two women in senior-level government positions, as deputy minister for women's education and general supervisor for women's higher education, in addition to senior advisors in multiple ministries. The country had a number of female diplomats. Bureaucratic procedures largely restricted women working in the security services to employment in female prisons, at women's universities, and in clerical positions in police stations where they were responsible for visually identifying other women for law enforcement purposes.

There are no laws that prevent male minorities from participating in political life on the same basis as other male citizens, but societal discrimination marginalized the Shia population. While the religious affiliation of Consultative Council members was not known publicly, the council included an estimated seven or eight Shia members. There were no known religious minorities in the cabinet. Multiple municipal councils in the Eastern Province, where most Shia are concentrated, had large proportions of Shia as members to reflect the local population, including a majority in Qatif and 50 percent in al-Hasa. At year's end there were some Eastern Province Shia judges dealing with intra-Shia personal status and family laws.

Section 4. Corruption and Lack of Transparency in Government

The law provides criminal penalties for official corruption. The government did not implement the law effectively, some officials engaged in corrupt practices with impunity, and perceptions of corruption persisted in some sectors.

Government employees who accept bribes face 10 years in prison or fines up to one million riyals ($267,000). The National Anticorruption Commission (Nazaha), established by the king in 2011, was responsible for promoting transparency and combating all forms of financial and administrative corruption. The commission was resourced adequately and issued numerous publications and undertook awareness campaigns on the religious necessity to combat corruption, both governmental and business. The commission's ministerial-level director reported directly to the king. In November the commission reported that it received approximately 100 reports per day; the commission investigated these reports and then forwarded relevant cases and its findings to the CIB and the BIP for appropriate action. During the year the commission actively campaigned against corruption and had a hotline for reporting such abuses. The CIB, however, remains responsible for investigating financial malfeasance, and the BIP has the lead on all criminal investigations. On September 15, the Consultative Council's Human Rights Committee criticized the Nazaha for the organization's failure to respond to the complaints made by citizens against many agencies under its jurisdiction. The Human Rights Council also responded to and researched complaints of corruption. Provincial governors and other members of the royal family paid compensation to victims of corruption during weekly majlis meetings where citizens raised complaints.

Corruption: On April 29, authorities sentenced Eissa al-Nekhaify to a three-year prison term, to be followed by a four-year travel ban, for "distorting the reputation" of Deputy Governor of Jazan Abdullah al-Suwayid by accusing the latter of corruption. Authorities charged al-Nekhaify after he publicly faulted the Ministry of Interior for covering up alleged instances of corruption in Jazan. Al-Nekhaify claimed that corrupt officials were responsible for the failure to provide compensation to citizens dislocated from the southern border with Yemen as a result of the 2009-10 military operation against the Houthis in Yemen. On November 24, an appeals court judge increased al-Nekhaify's sentence by eight months.

In March authorities convicted a senior official from the Jeddah municipality of accepting a bribe, fined him 700,000 riyals ($186,670), and sentenced him to five years in prison. The verdict was part of investigations and trials of municipal officials and others accused of corruption because of 2009 and 2011 Jeddah floods. At year's end a number of other trials related to corruption or misuse of position in connection with the Jeddah floods continued.

<u>Whistleblower Protection</u>: The law does not provide sufficient protection to public and private employees making internal disclosures or lawful public disclosures of evidence of illegality, such as the solicitation of bribes or other corrupt acts, gross waste or fraud, gross mismanagement, abuse of power, or substantial dangers to public health and safety.

<u>Financial Disclosure</u>: Public officials were not subject to financial disclosure laws.

<u>Public Access to Information</u>: The law does not provide for, and there is no right to, public access to government information, such as ministerial budgets or allocations to members of the royal family.

Section 5. Governmental Attitude Regarding International and Nongovernmental Investigation of Alleged Violations of Human Rights

The government did not allow international human rights NGOs to be based in the country but allowed representatives to visit on a limited basis. There were no transparent standards governing visits from international NGO representatives. The law provides that "the State shall protect human rights in accordance with the Islamic sharia"; however, the government restricted the activities of, while at times cooperating to varying degrees with, domestic and international human rights organizations in investigations of alleged violations of human rights.

The government often cooperated with and sometimes accepted the recommendations of the NSHR, the sole government-licensed domestic human rights organization. The NSHR accepted requests for assistance and complaints about government actions affecting human rights.

The government viewed unlicensed human rights groups with suspicion, frequently blocking their websites and threatening their founders with legal action (including ACPRA) and claimed they meddled in government affairs. The government continued to permit the informal operation of the Adala Center for Human Rights (a human rights NGO based in the Eastern Province), but since the group was formally "unlicensed," it remained unclear which activities the group could undertake without risking punishment. Without a license the group was unable to raise operating funds legally, which limited its activities. ACPRA applied for a license in 2008, which was not granted; however, the government allowed its unlicensed operation.

The HRC stated that the government welcomed the visits of legitimate, unbiased human rights groups, but added that the government could not act on the "hundreds of requests," in part because it was cumbersome to decide which domestic agency would be their interlocutor.

In August a court in Dammam in the Eastern Province dismissed a lawsuit by the founders of the Adala Center against the Ministry of Social Affairs for failing to license the NGO. Later in August the courts rejected the group's petition for an appeal. The ministry successfully argued that its refusal to license the Adala Center, which had operated since 2011, was lawful on the basis that the ministry is permitted under law to register only NGOs that are philanthropic or charitable in nature. The court decision also said the Adala Center's charter and governing documents were incompatible with the law because they referred to international law, including the Universal Declaration of Human Rights. Despite the outcome of the case, as of year's end the Adala Center continued to operate, although one of its founders, Fadhil al-Manasif, remained in detention. In September the BIP charged al-Manasif with a number of offenses including "participation in the formation of the illicit organization 'the Human Rights Activists' Network,' a related Eastern Province human rights group. On November 27, the presiding judge in al-Manasif's case indefinitely postponed the date of the judicial hearing in order to allow the BIP to bring additional charges against al-Manasif. As of year's end, al-Manasif remained in detention awaiting sentencing in the case.

On March 9, at the conclusion of the trial of Mohammed al-Qahtani and Abdullah al-Hamid, a Riyadh criminal court ordered the immediate dissolution of ACPRA along with the confiscation of its assets and the closure of its website and social media accounts.

On April 30, the founders of the Saudi Union for Human Rights, Abdullah Modhi al-Atawi, Mohammed Ayed al-Otaibi, Abdullah Faisal Badrani, and Mohammed Abdullah al-Otaibi, "suspended" the operation of their organization after they were brought in for questioning by the BIP in connection with "establishing an unlicensed organization." BIP officers reportedly told the group they could be sentenced to three to four years in prison for this crime unless they immediately agreed to "freeze the activity of the organization" less than a month after it was founded.

Government Human Rights Bodies: The HRC is part of the government and requires the permission of the Ministry of Foreign Affairs before meeting with foreign diplomats, academics, or researchers with international human rights organizations. The HRC president has ministerial status and reports to the king. According to the NSHR's 2009 report, the HRC "met with weak collaboration on the part of some governmental bodies in spite of the issuance of royal directives." The well-resourced HRC was effective in highlighting problems and registering and responding to complaints received, but its capacity to effect change was more limited. The HRC worked directly with the Royal Diwan and the Council of Ministers; with a committee composed of representatives of the Consultative Council and the Ministries of Labor, Social Affairs, and Interior; and with Consultative Council Committees for the Judiciary, Islamic Affairs, and Human Rights. During the year the HRC and NSHR were more outspoken in areas deemed less politically sensitive, including child abuse, child marriage, and prison conditions. They avoided topics such as protests, indefinite detentions, or cases of political activists or reformists that would require directly confronting government authorities. The HRC board's membership included at least three Shia of 19 full-time members; they received and responded to complaints submitted to them by their constituencies, including issues related to religious freedom and women's rights. The Consultative Council's Human Rights Committee also actively followed cases and included women and Shia among its members; a woman served as deputy chairman of the committee.

Section 6. Discrimination, Societal Abuses, and Trafficking in Persons

The law prohibits discrimination based on race but not gender, disability, language, sexual orientation and gender identity, or social status. The law and tradition discriminate based on gender. The law and the guardianship system restrict women to the status of a legal dependent vis-a-vis their male guardians. This status is unchanged even after women reach adulthood. Women and some men faced widespread and state-enforced segregation based on societal, cultural, and religious traditions.

The government generally reinforced sharia-based traditional prohibitions on discrimination based on disability, language, social status, or race.

Women

Rape and Domestic Violence: Rape is a criminal offense under sharia with a wide range of penalties from flogging to execution. The government enforced the law based on its interpretation of sharia, and courts punished victims as well as perpetrators for illegal "mixing of genders," even when there was no conviction for rape. Consequently, due to the legal and social penalties, authorities brought few cases to trial. The government did not recognize spousal rape. Statistics on incidents of rape were not available, but press reports and observers indicated rape was a serious problem. The government did not maintain public records on prosecutions, convictions, or punishments. Most rape cases were unreported because victims faced societal reprisal, diminished marriage opportunities, criminal sanction up to imprisonment, or accusations of adultery.

On August 26, the Council of Ministers announced the adoption of a law against domestic abuse, which defines domestic abuse and provides a framework for the government to prevent and protect victims of abuse. The new law criminalizes domestic abuse with penalties of one month to one year of imprisonment and/or a fine of between 5,000 and 50,000 riyals ($1,330-$13,330) unless a court provides a harsher sentence.

Researchers stated that domestic violence may be seriously underreported, making it difficult to gauge the magnitude of the problem, which they believed to be widespread. Independent estimates supported by officials working at the Ministry of Social Affairs indicated that the incidence of female spousal abuse ranged widely, from 16 to 50 percent of all wives. Officials stated that the government did not clearly define domestic violence and that procedures concerning cases, and thus enforcement, varied from one government body to another. The NSHR's 2011 annual report noted that the organization investigated 370 cases of domestic violence and violations of women's rights, compared with 282 such cases in 2010. Noting that family violence was an increasing problem, the Ministry of Social Affairs reported that the number of family violence incidents against women in 2011 reached 931 cases. Violence included a broad spectrum of abuse. There were reports of police or judges returning women directly to their abusers, most of whom were the women's legal guardians. The government made efforts to combat domestic violence, and the King Abdulaziz Center for National Dialogue held workshops and distributed educational materials on peaceful conflict resolution between spouses and in families.

The government supported family protection shelters. The HRC received complaints of domestic abuse and referred these complaints to other government offices. During 2011, the most recent year comprehensive statistics on domestic violence were available, the HRC's women and children's branches throughout the kingdom received 350 complaints, including 71 from women; domestic violence and abuse accounted for most cases. The HRC advised complainants and offered legal assistance to some female litigants. The organization provided facilities for children of women complainants and litigants, and it distributed publications supporting women's rights in education, health care, development, and the workplace.

Sexual Harassment: The extent of sexual harassment was difficult to measure with little media reporting and no government data. The government's interpretation of sharia guides courts on cases of sexual harassment. Employers in many sectors maintained separate male and female workspaces where feasible.

Reproductive Rights: There were no reports of government interference in a couple's right to decide freely and responsibly the number, spacing, and timing of children and to have the information and means to do so free from discrimination, coercion, and violence. Prenatal care, essential obstetric care, and postpartum care were available, but patients were not always aware of its availability, and medical staff did not always emphasize its importance. Intrauterine devices were the most popular form of birth control, and women, regardless of marital status, were legally able to obtain them. Birth control pills also were available to women in local pharmacies without prescriptions. Although no legal barriers prevented access to contraception, constraints on mobility and economic resources as well as social pressure for large families limited many women. Information was not available regarding equal diagnosis and treatment of sexually transmitted infections.

Discrimination: Women continued to face significant discrimination under law and custom, and many remained uninformed about their unequal rights. Although they may legally own property and are entitled to financial support from their guardian, women have fewer political or social rights than men, and society treats them as unequal members in the political and social spheres. The country's interpretation of sharia prohibits women from marrying non-Muslims, but men may marry Christians and Jews. Women require government permission to marry noncitizens; men must obtain government permission if they intend to marry noncitizens from countries other than Gulf Cooperation Council member states Bahrain, Kuwait, Oman, Qatar, and the United Arab Emirates. Women do not directly transmit citizenship to their children.

The guardianship system requires that every woman have a close male relative as her "guardian" with the legal authority to approve her travel outside of the country. A guardian also has authority to approve some types of business licenses and study at a university or college. Women can make their own determinations concerning hospital care. Women can work without their guardian's permission; however, most employers required women have their guardian's permission. A husband who "verbally" (rather than via a court process) divorces his wife or refuses to sign final divorce papers continues to be her legal guardian. The law does not require equal pay for equal work.

Widespread societal exclusion enforced by, but not limited to, state institutions restricted women from using many public facilities. The law requires women usually to sit in separate, specially designated family sections. They frequently cannot consume food in restaurants that do not have such sections. Women risk arrest for riding in a private vehicle driven by a male who is not an employee (such as a hired chauffeur or taxi driver) or a close male relative. Cultural norms enforced by state institutions require women to wear an abaya (a loose-fitting, full-length black cloak) in public. The CPVPV also generally expected Muslim women to cover their hair and non-Muslim women from Asian and African countries to comply more fully with local customs of dress than non-Muslim Western women. In some rural areas and smaller cities, women adhered to the traditional dress code covering the entire body, including hands, feet, hair, and face.

Women also faced discrimination in courts, where the testimony of one man equals that of two women. All judges are male, and women faced restriction on their practice of law. In divorce proceedings women must demonstrate legally specified grounds for divorce, but men can divorce without giving cause. In doing so, men must pay immediately an amount of money agreed at the time of the marriage that serves as a one-time alimony payment; however, men can be forced to make subsequent alimony payments by court order. Women who demonstrate legal grounds for divorce are entitled to alimony.

Women faced discrimination under family law. For example, a woman needs a guardian's permission to marry or must seek a court order in the case of adhl (male guardians refusing to approve the marriage of women under their charge). In such adhl cases, the judge assumes the role of the guardian and can approve the marriage. Courts award custody of children when they attain a specified age (seven years for boys and nine years for girls) to the divorced husband or the deceased husband's family. In numerous cases former husbands prevented divorced noncitizen women from visiting their children. Inheritance laws also discriminate against women, since daughters receive half the inheritance awarded to their brothers.

According to recent surveys, women constituted more than half of university students; however, segregated education through university level was the norm. The only exceptions to segregation in higher education were medical schools at the undergraduate level and the King Abdullah University of Science and Technology, a graduate-level research university, where women worked jointly with men, were not required to wear the veil, and drove cars on campus. Other universities, such as al-Faisal University in Riyadh, offered partially segregated classes with students receiving instruction from the same teacher and able to participate together in class discussion, but with the women and men physically separated by dividers.

The Ministry of Labor explicitly approves and encourages the employment of women in specific sectors.

In 2011 the Ministry of Labor issued regulations requiring all stores selling women's undergarments and cosmetics to be staffed solely by women. In November 2012 the ministry announced implementation of this regulation. As of year's end, however, the government had not universally applied the regulations, either in urban neighborhoods habituated by foreign noncitizen workers or outside major cities. On July 21, the government acknowledged that efforts to implement regulations to employ Saudi women in this sector were still in progress. The 2011 regulations also ban women from 20 professions, mostly in heavy industry, but create guidelines for women to telework. In November 2012 the Board of Grievances began recruiting women to work in its judicial offices across the country answering inquiries, registering cases, delivering copies of verdicts, and checking the identity of female clients. A 2010 report by the central bank estimated that 36,000 female citizens worked in the public sector and 48,000 in the private sector, in a total labor force of more than nine million. The vast majority of the 1.4 million women working in the kingdom were foreign laborers with significant additional restrictions on their rights. There were cases during the year of women workers fleeing their sponsors because of reported abuse.

Widespread gender segregation and societal pressures directly led to discrimination in employment. Despite gender segregation, the law grants women the right to obtain business licenses with the approval of their guardians, and women frequently obtained licenses in fields that might require them to supervise foreign workers, interact with male clients, or deal with government officials. In medical settings and in the energy industry, women and men worked together, and in some instances women supervised male employees. Women who work in establishments with 50 or more female employees have the right to maternity leave and childcare.

Children

Birth Registration: Citizenship derives from the father, and only the father can register a birth. There were cases of children of citizen parents being denied public services, including education and health care, because the government failed independently to register the birth entirely or immediately, sometimes due to the failure of the father to report the birth.

Child Abuse: Abuse of children occurred, but information was sparse. In 2012 the NSHR registered 79 instances of violence against children, according to its annual report, compared with 95 instances in 2011.

On October 7, Fayhan al-Ghamdi, a former television preacher accused of torturing to death his five-year-old daughter, Lama, was sentenced to eight years in prison, 600 lashes, and a remunerative payment (diyah, or blood money) of three million riyals ($800,000) to the girl's mother in compensation for her death. The HRC provided Lama's mother with free legal counsel during the case.

Forced and Early Marriage: There were reports during the year of child marriage, although it was almost entirely limited to rural areas. Senior government officials spoke out against the practice and advocated the adoption of a minimum marriage age. Sharia does not specify a minimum age for marriage but suggests girls may marry after reaching puberty. According to some senior religious leaders, girls as young as age 10 may be married. Families sometimes arranged such marriages, principally in rural areas or to settle family debts, without the consent of the child. The HRC and NSHR monitored cases of child marriages, which they reported were rare or, at least, rarely reported. The bride's age must be recorded in the application for a marriage license, and registration of the marriage is a legal prerequisite for consummation. The government reportedly instructed marriage registrars not to register marriages involving children.

Sexual Exploitation of Children: The Anti-Cyber Crimes Law stipulates that imprisonment and fines for crimes including the preparation, publication, and promotion of material for pornographic sites may be no less than two and one-half years' imprisonment or 1.5 million riyals ($400,000) if the crime includes the exploitation of minors. The law does not define a minimum age for consensual sex.

International Child Abduction: The kingdom is not a party to the 1980 Hague Convention on the Civil Aspects of International Child Abduction.

Anti-Semitism

There were no known Jewish citizens and no statistics available concerning the religious denominations of foreigners.

According to the Ministry of Islamic Affairs, no imams publicly espoused intolerant views warranting dismissal during the year. In contrast with previous years, there were no reports that Sunni imams, who receive government stipends, used anti-Jewish, anti-Christian, or anti-Shia language in their sermons. During the year the ministry issued periodic circulars to clerics and imams in mosques directing them to include messages on the principles of justice, equality, and tolerance and to encourage rejection of bigotry and all forms of racial discrimination in their sermons.

The government's multi-year "Tatweer" project to revise textbooks, curricula, and teaching methods to promote tolerance and remove content disparaging religions other than Islam began in 2007. As of year's end, the program had benefitted from more than 11 billion riyals ($2.9 billion) in spending to revise the curriculum. At year's end new curricula and textbooks had been developed for at least grades four through 10; however, despite these efforts, some intolerant material remained in textbooks used in schools.

Editorial cartoons occasionally exhibited anti-Semitism characterized by stereotypical images of Jews along with Jewish symbols, particularly at times of heightened political tension with Israel. Anti-Semitic comments by journalists, academics, and clerics occasionally appeared in the media.

Trafficking in Persons

See the Department of State's *Trafficking in Persons Report* at www.state.gov/j/tip.

Persons with Disabilities

The law does not prohibit discrimination against persons with physical, sensory, intellectual, and mental disabilities in employment, education, air travel and other transportation, access to health care, or the provision of other state services or other areas. The law does not require public accessibility to buildings, information, and communications. Newer commercial buildings often included such access, as did some newer government buildings. Children with disabilities could attend government-supported schools. Persons with disabilities had equal access to information and communications.

Information about patterns of abuse of persons with disabilities in prisons and educational and mental health institutions was not widely available. Persons with disabilities could participate in civic affairs, and there are no restrictions on men with disabilities from voting in Municipal Council elections. During the year the HRC appointed four subject matter experts to work as advocates for persons with disabilities in the kingdom and to respond to complaints of discrimination. The Prince Salman Center for Disability Research, a nonprofit research foundation, continued to conduct laboratory and field research on a range of disability and quality of life issues. The Ministry of Social Affairs is responsible for protecting the rights of persons with disabilities. Vocational rehabilitation projects and social care programs increasingly brought persons with disabilities into the mainstream.

National/Racial/Ethnic Minorities

Although racial discrimination is illegal, societal discrimination against members of national, racial, and ethnic minorities was a problem. There was also discrimination based on tribal or nontribal lineage. There was formal and informal discrimination, especially racial discrimination against foreign workers from Africa and Asia. The tolerance campaign of the King Abdulaziz Center for National Dialogue sought to address some of these problems, and it provided training during the year to combat discrimination against national, racial, or ethnic groups.

There were numerous cases of assault against foreign workers and reports of widespread worker abuse. The Shia minority continued to suffer social, legal, economic, and political discrimination. To address the problem, in recent years the Ministries of Defense and Interior and the National Guard held antidiscrimination training courses run by the King Abdulaziz Center for National Dialogue for police and law enforcement officers

Societal Abuses, Discrimination, and Acts of Violence Based on Sexual Orientation and Gender Identity

Under sharia, as interpreted in the country, consensual same-sex sexual conduct is punishable by death or flogging, depending on the perceived seriousness of the case. It is illegal for men "to behave like women" or to wear women's clothes, and vice versa. Due to social conventions and potential persecution, lesbian, gay, bisexual, and transgender organizations did not operate openly, nor were there gay rights advocacy events of any kind. There were reports of official societal discrimination, physical violence, and harassment based on sexual orientation or gender identity in employment, housing, statelessness, access to education, or health care. Stigma or intimidation was likely to limit reports of incidents of abuse. Sexual orientation and gender identity could constitute the basis for harassment, blackmail, or other actions.

In April 2012 authorities announced "gays, tomboys, and emos" would not be allowed to enter public schools and universities until they changed their "appearance and behavior." The CPVPV announced receiving high-level orders to enforce these new rules on "girls who adopt masculine appearances" and those emulating the "emo" subculture.

There were no government efforts to address potential discrimination.

Other Societal Violence or Discrimination

There was no reported societal violence or discrimination against persons with HIV/AIDS. By law the government deported foreign workers who tested positive for HIV/AIDS upon arrival or when hospitalized for other reasons. There was no indication that HIV-positive foreigners failed to receive antiretroviral treatment or that authorities isolated them during the year. The Ministry of Health's HIV/AIDS program worked to fight stigma and discrimination against persons with HIV/AIDS.

Section 7. Worker Rights

a. Freedom of Association and the Right to Collective Bargaining

The law does not provide for the right of workers to form and join independent unions. The law does not protect the right to collective bargaining or the right to conduct legal strikes. The law does not protect against antiunion discrimination or require reinstatement of workers fired for union activity.

There are no labor unions in the country, and workers face potential dismissal, imprisonment, or, in the case of migrant workers, deportation for union activities. The Commission for the Settlement of Labor Disputes under the Ministry of Labor investigates labor-related complaints by private individuals against officials responsible for the enforcement of the provisions of the laws.

The government allows citizen-only labor committees in workplaces with more than 100 employees, but it places undue limitations on freedom of association and is heavily involved in the formation and activities of these committees. For example, the Ministry of Labor approves the committee members and authorizes ministry and employer representatives to attend committee meetings. The minutes of the meetings must be submitted to management and then transmitted to the minister; the ministry can dissolve committees if they violate regulations or are deemed to threaten public security. Committees are limited to making recommendations to company management regarding only improvements to work conditions, health and safety, productivity, and training programs. In its 2012 annual report, the NSHR registered 329 labor-related complaints.

The government did not respect freedom of association and the right to collective bargaining.

b. Prohibition of Forced or Compulsory Labor

The law prohibits forced or compulsory labor; however, the government did not effectively enforce legal protections for migrant workers. Forced labor occurred, especially among migrant workers, notably domestic servants, and children. Conditions indicative of forced labor experienced by foreign workers included withholding of passports, nonpayment of wages, restrictions on movement, and verbal, physical, and sexual abuse; however, during the year the government announced changes to the labor law designed to stop these abuses. Many noncitizen workers, particularly domestic employees, were not able to exercise their right to end their contractual work. Restrictive sponsorship laws increased workers' vulnerability to forced labor conditions and made many foreign workers reluctant to report abuse.

Throughout the year the government strictly implemented measures to limit the number of illegal noncitizen workers in the kingdom, repatriating approximately one million foreign nationals; these included approximately 300,000 Yemeni nationals, the largest single group of noncitizen laborers in the country, and more than 100,000 Ethiopians. The government also penalized haj tourist agencies that engaged in human trafficking and Saudi companies that abused the country's visa laws to bring individuals into the country for reasons other than to employ them directly. A government campaign between April and November to correct the legal status of noncitizen laborers by transferring their sponsorship or deporting them resulted in many noncitizen workers leaving the country. As of year's end, an estimated two to three million foreigners resided illegally in the country;

authorities believed many of them illegally transited the border with Yemen. Many also either left their legal sponsors' employment or stayed on after expiration of their work visas and residence permits. A smaller number came as religious pilgrims and overstayed their visas. As a consequence of their illegal status, these individuals were susceptible to forced labor, substandard wages, and deportation by authorities amid a major crackdown on undocumented laborers that began in November.

In November, after authorities announced the end of an amnesty period for illegal foreign workers to correct their status or depart the country, security forces resumed arrests of undocumented noncitizen workers. Violence that coincided with the deportation campaign resulted in the death of at least three persons, including a police officer struck in the head with a rock and an Ethiopian man who was shot. Subsequent riots injured at least 68 persons. Police alleged that noncitizen workers resisted arrest and were carrying weapons. Many deported laborers returned to their countries of origin destitute, and some complained of poor treatment and abuse by authorities or fellow detainees during the deportation process.

Also see the Department of State's *Trafficking in Persons Report* at www.state.gov/j/tip.

c. Prohibition of Child Labor and Minimum Age for Employment

The law states no person younger than 15 years old may legally work unless that person is the sole source of support for the family. Children between 13 and 15 may work if the job is not harmful to health or growth and does not interfere with schooling. The law states that legal minors may not be employed in hazardous operations or harmful industries; children under 18 may not be employed for shifts exceeding six hours a day. There is no minimum age for workers employed in family-owned businesses or other areas considered extensions of the household, such as farming, herding, and domestic service.

The HRC and the NSHR are responsible for monitoring the enforcement of the country's child labor laws. There was little information on government efforts to enforce relevant laws or actions to prevent or eliminate child labor during the year. The most common enforcement of the law was in response to complaints of children begging on the streets.

Child labor occurred, most commonly in the form of children, usually from other countries including Yemen and Ethiopia, forced into child begging rings, street vending, and work in family businesses. Although in previous years there were reports of foreign domestic workers younger than 18 (some of whom reportedly traveled to the country with forged documents), such abuses could not be confirmed during the year.

d. Acceptable Conditions of Work

The monthly minimum wage for public sector employees was 3,000 riyals ($800). There was no private sector minimum wage for foreign workers; however, the government's Nitaqaat (Saudization) program set a general minimum wage for citizens at 3,000 riyals ($800) per month.

The Commission for the Settlement of Labor Disputes actively prosecuted cases against employers of citizens, with most cases favoring the employee. Prosecution of employers of noncitizens occurred with less frequency, and most verdicts reportedly favored the employer. Labor regulations ostensibly apply to all workers in the public and private sector other than domestic servants (covered by a separate law). The regulations provide for a 48-hour standard workweek at regular pay, a weekly 24-hour rest period (normally on Fridays, although the employer may grant it on another day), and time-and-a-half pay for overtime, with a maximum of 12 additional hours per week. The regulations do not distinguish between different types of employment. The law's provisions were not enforced.

In August the Council of Ministers approved new regulations to govern the work relationship between employers and domestic workers, including the creation of a dispute mechanism to settle and adjudicate financial claims. Under the new regulations, the employer and the employee must have a written agreement outlining the worker's duties and rights that would then be subjected to legal action should either party fail to uphold the contract. If an employer commits a violation, the punishment could include a one-year recruitment ban, a 2,000 riyal ($530) fine, or both, with increasing penalties for repeat offenses. Domestic workers violating their contract could be assessed a similar fine and be prohibited from working in the kingdom.

In April 2012 the Ministry of Labor announced the creation of 1,000 additional labor inspector positions to investigate labor law violations. As of April, 600 inspectors had been hired. According to the Ministry of Labor, the remaining 400 inspectors would be women. The law penalizes individuals between 500 riyals

($133) and 1,000 riyals ($267) for bringing foreigners into the country to work in any service, including domestic service, without following the required procedures and obtaining a permit.

The labor law provides for regular safety inspections and enables Ministry of Labor-appointed inspectors to examine materials used or handled in industrial and other operations and to submit samples of suspected hazardous materials or substances to government laboratories. The Ministry of Health's Occupational Health Service Directorate works with the Ministry of Labor on health and safety matters. Regulations require employers to protect some workers from job-related hazards and disease, although some violations occurred. These regulations did not cover farmers, herdsmen, domestic servants, or workers in family-operated businesses. Foreign nationals privately reported frequent failures to enforce health and safety standards.

The law requires that foreign workers be sponsored by a citizen or business to obtain legal work and residency status. During the six-month "grace period" from April to November, noncitizen workers could change their workplace and sponsorship without their previous sponsor's permission. Previously, the government also lifted restrictions to allow noncitizen workers to switch from their current employers to employers or companies that employed a sufficient quota of Saudi nationals. Despite these revised restrictions, some workers remained uninformed of the changed regulations and had to stay with their current sponsor until fulfillment of the contract or seek the assistance of their embassy to return home. There were also instances in which sponsors bringing noncitizen workers into the country failed to provide them with a residency permit, which undermined their ability to access government services or navigate the court system in the event of grievances. Sponsors with commercial or labor disputes with foreign employees also could ask authorities to prohibit the employees from departing the country until the dispute was resolved.

The Ministry of Labor's Migrant Workers' Welfare Department is responsible for addressing cases of abuse and exploitation among migrant workers. Noncitizen workers were able to submit complaints and seek help from the 37 offices throughout the country, although the government was generally unresponsive. The Ministry of Labor reportedly maintained a database of abusive employers and occasionally banned individuals and companies who mistreated noncitizen workers from sponsoring such workers for up to five years; however, the ministry did not provide any examples of employers banned during the year.

Bilateral labor agreements set conditions on foreign workers' minimum wage, housing, benefits including leave and medical care, and other topics. These provisions were not necessarily drafted with reference to international standards, and they varied depending on the sending country's relative bargaining leverage. The labor law and the 2009 law against trafficking provide penalties for abuse of such workers.

During 2011 the governments of Indonesia and the Philippines banned new domestic workers from working in the country while they sought improved contract terms for their citizens. The Philippines also requested that prospective employers provide bank statements. At year's end the Indonesian ban remained in place. In May, however, the Saudi and Philippine governments concluded a bilateral work agreement, and Philippine officials lifted the ban, allowing Philippine domestic workers to deploy to the kingdom for the first time since 2011. As part of the agreement, the government agreed to enforce a minimum wage of 1,500 riyals ($400) per month and again committed to prevent contract substitution and the seizure of workers' passports.

In 2011 the Ministry of Labor mandated the establishment of fewer and larger expatriate labor recruitment firms, ostensibly better to protect migrant workers, including domestic workers. As of year's end, the ministry registered 13 unified recruitment firms, each of which will have an office in each of the country's 13 provinces.

The government engaged in a news campaign highlighting the plight of abused workers, trained law enforcement and other officials on combating trafficking in persons, and worked with the embassies of labor-sending countries to disseminate information about labor rights to foreign workers. During Ramadan the HRC broadcast a public awareness program on television emphasizing the Islamic injunction to treat employees well.

An estimated eight million noncitizen workers, including approximately 1.5 million female domestic employees, made up the majority of the country's labor force. Legal workers generally negotiated and agreed to conditions prior to arrival in the country, in accordance with the contract requirements contained in the labor law; nevertheless, many found themselves subjected to different conditions, such as delays in payment of wages, changes in employer, or changed working hours and conditions. Migrant workers, especially domestic workers, were vulnerable to abuse, exploitation, and conditions contravening labor laws, including nonpayment of wages, working for periods in excess of the 48-hour week, working for periods longer than the prescribed eight-hour workday, and restrictions on movement due to passport confiscation. There were also reports of physical and verbal abuse. The labor regulations announced in August seek to reduce instances of such abuse. The law's new requirements include transferring wages by direct deposit in the bank account of the employee to ensure documentation of the payment of wages. Moreover, the Ministry of Labor must have on file a fixed postal address for each sponsor of a noncitizen employee.

Many noncitizen workers, particularly domestic employees, were not able to exercise their right to remove themselves from dangerous situations. Some employers physically prevented workers from leaving or threatened them with nonpayment of wages if they left. Sponsoring employers, who controlled foreign workers' ability to remain employed and in the country, usually held foreign workers' passports, a practice prohibited by law. In some contract disputes, a sponsor held the employee in country until resolution of the dispute to force the employee to accept a disadvantageous settlement or risk deportation without any settlement.

Foreign workers could contact the labor offices of their embassies for assistance. During the year hundreds of domestic workers sought shelter at their embassies, some fleeing sexual abuse or other violence by their employers. Some embassies maintained safe houses for citizens fleeing situations that amounted to bondage. The workers usually sought legal help from embassies and government agencies to obtain end of service benefits and exit visas.

In addition to their embassies, domestic employees may contact the NSHR, the HRC, the governmental interministerial General Secretariat to Combat Human Trafficking, and the Ministry of Labor's Migrant Workers' Welfare Department, which provided services to safeguard migrant workers' rights and to protect them from abuse. Workers may also apply to the offices of regional governors and may lodge an appeal with the Board of Grievances against decisions from those authorities.